This Book Belongs To _____

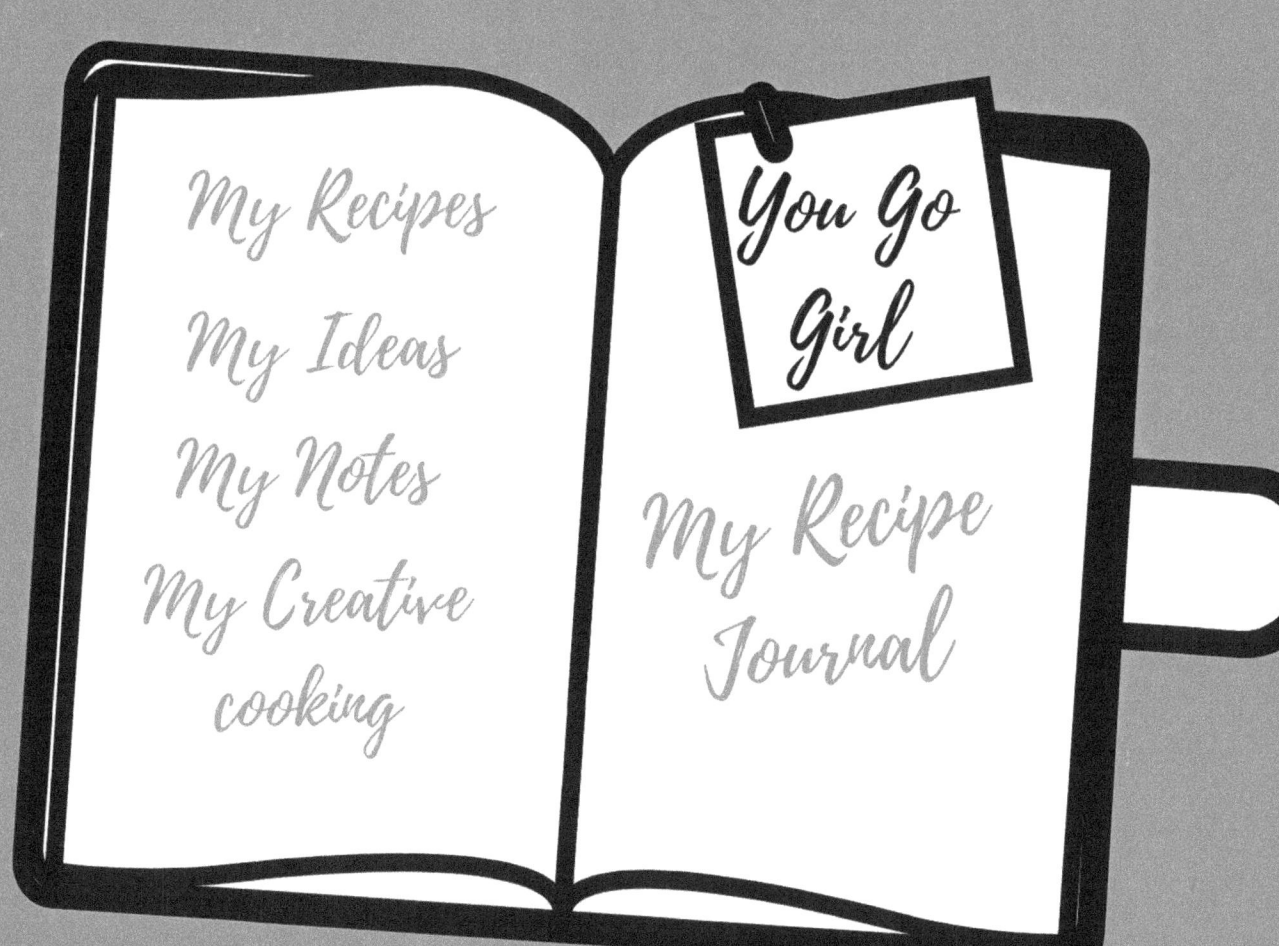

FOR THE LOVE OF FOOD

WHO SAYS *Cute girls* CAN'T COOK?

a recipe food journal

Jamila LaCosta

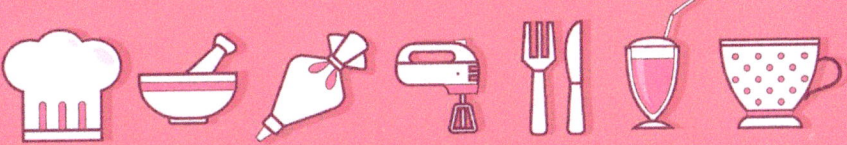

WHO SAYS CUTE GIRLS CAN'T COOK? Copyright © 2020. Jamila LaCosta

All rights reserved. No part of this publication may be reproduced, distributed, or transmitted in any form or by any means, including photocopying, recording, or other electronic or mechanical methods, without the prior written permission of the publisher or author.

LaCosta Publishing House

ISBN: 978-1-949343-91-5 (hardback)

978-1-949343-92-2 (paperback)

Printed in the United States of America

Introduction

Every Foodie has their favorite recipe and their favorite food dish. Saving recipes is a wonderful tradition, but it can be difficult to keep them organized and in one place. You may have them printed from your laptop or they may have been handed down from generations. This food journal is the perfect place to arrange and store your favorite recipes.

The organization is up to you.

You can place them in alphabetical order, by the season, by the places you travel, whatever method you choose, this journal will keep all your recipes together and in excellent condition. This journal also provides some helpful hints & tips for a variety of topics: cooking terms & methods, baking secrets, grilling tips, wine facts and so much more.

HOW MUCH OF THIS EQUALS THAT

1/2 cup of uncooked noodles = 1 cup cooked

25 mushrooms = 6 cups sliced

2 garlic cloves = 1 tsp

1 medium lime = 2 tablespoons

2 tbsp of popcorn kernels = 4 cups popped

1 can of condensed milk = 1 1/4 cups

215 grams of sugar = 2 1/2 cups

1 can of chicken broth = 1 3/4 cups

4 oz of almonds = 1 cup

18 oz package of cream cheese = 1 cup

1 pound of flour = 4 cups

1 medium apple = 1 cup slice

"MEASURE WITH LOVE"

SUBSTITUTE THAT

IF YOU DON'T HAVE — **USE THIS**

- 1 cup of honey → 1/4 cups of granulated sugar plus 1/4 cup of water
- 1 tbsp of vinegar → 2 tbsp of lemon or lemon juice
- 1/2 cup of olive oil → 1 cup of butter

"Omit & substitute! That's how recipes should be written

IS IT DONE?

BAKED GOODS

Muffins
- until golden brown
- until no wet batter on the toothpick
- until cake starts to pull away

Cakes & Cupcakes
- until toothpick inserted into center comes out clean
- until cake starts to pull away

Casseroles
- until hot & bubbly
- until heated thoroughly
- until cheese melts

Cookies
- until lightly browned
- until edges are golden brown

IS IT DONE?

MEAT

Lamb
- well done 155°F
- medium 140°F

Pork
- medium 145°F

Beef (roast or steak)
- medium 135°F
- well done 160°F

Poultry
- until chicken is no longer pink with a crispy brown color

IS IT DONE?

VARIETIES

Sauces
- until thickened

Soups
- until heated through

VEGGIES
- until crisp tender

SEAFOOD

Clams
- until clams open

Fish
- until fish begins to flake

Shrimp
- until shrimp are pink & opaque

Scallops
- until opaque

STEWS
- until meat is tender
- until veggies are tender

Wash hands with hot soapy water before handling and preparing food. Rewash them after touching your mouth, your nose or carrying your children around. Do not cough or sneeze on food during preparation.

To avoid contaminating other foods, wash hands after raw poultry, meat, seafood or eggs. Thoroughly wash any cutting surfaces and utensils with hot, soapy water, if they been in contact with raw poultry, meat, seafood or eggs. This reduces the risk of being exposed to bacteria in raw foods. Salmonella and E. coli are killed during cooking.

Keep raw meat and poultry packages away from other food items, especially produce and unwrap items.

The juices from the raw food can drip and contaminate the other foods.

Cook food to the proper temperature. When testing for doneness, use a meat thermometer with meats and poultry.

Do not use the same pan or platter for both raw and cooked foods.

WHO SAYS CUTE GIRLS CAN'T COOK?

Regardless of the cooking methods used, always cook chicken completely.

Do not partially cook and then store poultry for further cooking.

Use clean, uncracked Grade A eggs, and cook the eggs until the yolks are thicken and set.

Rinse poultry and fish under cold running water to remove surface dirt and bone fragments.

Rinse fruits and vegetables, scrubbing with a brush to remove embedded soil, if necessary.

Organisms that cause food borne illness thrive at temperature between 40 F and 140 F. Thaw foods in the refrigerator rather than on the counter at room temperature.

At picnics and on buffet tables, keep hot food above a 140 F and cold foods below 40 F. Do not let cook food stand longer than two hours. Any cook food that has remained unrefrigerated for more than two hours must be discarded. Food should never sit out for more than one hour.

Chill leftovers quickly. Do not transfer a large pot of food directly from the oven to the refrigerator. Divide it into several containers so that it will chill quickly.

Cooking Terms & Methods

Baste

The technique of brushing, spooning or pouring liquids over food, usually meat and poultry as it cooks. It helps preserve moistness, adds flavor, and gives food an attractive appearance.

Beat

The method of stirring or mixing vigorously.

Braise

A moist heat cooking method used to tenderize tough cuts of meat or fibrous vegetables.

Brown

The method of cooking food quickly until the surface is brown.

Caramelize

The technique of cooking sugar, sometimes with a small amount of water, to an extremely high temperature so that it melts into a clear brown liquid and develops a characteristic flavor.

Jamila LaCosta

Cream

The technique of mixing ingredients until light and fluffy.

Crisp

To refresh or to make firm and brittle.

Cut In

The method used to combine solid, cold fats, such as butter, with dry ingredients, such as flour. The results are small, coarse pieces.

Deglaze

The technique of adding liquid using water, wine or broth to a pan to loosen brown food particles.

Dice

To cut food into small square pieces.

Dust

To lightly coat food, before or after cooking with a powdery ingredient.

WHO SAYS CUTE GIRLS CAN'T COOK?

Fold

To incorporate one food or mixture into another.

Julienne

To cut vegetables into thin 4-sided strips.

Mince

To cut foods, such as onions and garlic, into exceptionally fine pieces.

Pare

To remove the thin outer covering or skin of a food, usually a fruit or vegetable.

Plump

To silk foods in any warmed liquid, allowing them to swell and soften by absorbing some of the liquid.

Poach

To cook food slowly and gently in a simmering, but not boiling, liquid that just covers the food.

Puree

To mash or strain soft cook food until it has a smooth consistency.

Sauté

To cook or brown food in a small amount of fat in a skillet or sauté pan.

Sear

Exposing meat to an extremely high heat to quickly brown the outside, while sealing the juices inside.

Simmer

Cooking food in a liquid, with gentle heat just below the boiling point.

Steep

Soaking a dry ingredient in a liquid that is usually hot in order to transfer its flavor and color to the liquid.

Whip

Beating ingredients, such as egg whites or whipping cream, with a wire whisk or electric mixer to incorporate air and increase volume.

Recipes are guidelines, it is up to the Cook to bring the

Ingredients 2 Life!

SPICE IT UP

DO YOU KNOW YOUR SPICE GAME

Herbs are great plants, as they have so many uses. Although most aromatic herbs can be used for cooking, sometimes the aroma is all you need. Herbs can sometimes be the primary ingredient in a recipe such as cilantro in tacos. Herbs can also be used in teas and food coloring.

Spices come from the seeds, bark, roots fruit, and flowers. They add flavor and color to both sweet and savory dishes.

When purchasing fresh herbs, look for brightly colored, fresh looking leaves without any brown spots. If a fresh herb is not available substitute it with the dry herb.

Storing your herbs and spices properly is important for future use. Buy fresh herbs in small quantity. Wash and place in a plastic bag and store in refrigerator. They will last between 3 to 5 days.

When you buy dry herbs and spices write the purchase date on the container and discard after 6 months. Heat and moisture will cause their flavor to deteriorate more quickly. Buy them in small quantities and store in a cool, dry place.

WHO SAYS CUTE GIRLS CAN'T COOK?

Basil

Is a member of the mint family and can be used fresh or dried. It is used in Italian dishes and pizza.

Chives

Are part of the onion family. They are used fresh. Chives add wonderful flavors to your recipes, such as salad, eggs, sauces, and dips.

Cilantro

Sometimes called Chinese parsley, are the leaves and stems of the coriander plant. It is used in Asian, Caribbean, and Latin dishes.

Oregano

Is a member of the mint family. It has a strong flavor and aroma. It is used in fresh and dried forms. There is a Mexican and an Italian variety.

Parsley

Is a popular herb; it is used a lot. Used fresh or dried. It has a mild flavor and is used well with fish dishes, sauces, meats, and vegetables.

Bay Leaves

Are mostly found in dried form. They are used for soups, stews and they must be removed before serving.

Marjoram

Is a member of the mint family and has mild, sweet, oregano-like flavor. It is used mostly in its dried form to flavor salads, sauces, cooked green vegetables, and meats.

Mint

Has over thirty varieties, but its most common types are peppermint and spearmint. Sold fresh or dried. Flavors Lamb, sweet & savory dishes, beverages, lamb, and cooked vegetables.

Thyme

Is part of the mint family. It has a lemon aroma and is used for stews, meats, and sauces.

Cinnamon

Comes from the inner bark. It is used in sweet dishes but can also flavor meat dishes, stews, and curries. Can be bought in whole sticks or ground form.

Cumin

Is available in whole seeds or ground. It is an ingredient in curry and chili powder. Cumin is often used in Latin, Middle Eastern, Asian, and in Mediterranean cooking.

WHO SAYS CUTE GIRLS CAN'T COOK?

Curry

Powder is a blend of many different spices, herbs, and seeds. The flavor can range from mild to spicy hot. It is used on fish and meats.

Cayenne

Red pepper is made from various tropical, dried chilies. It is used to add heat and spiciness to recipes.

Nutmeg

Is the seed from the nutmeg tree. Sold whole or ground. It is used in bake goods.

Paprika

Is a ground red spice ranging from mild to hot. Used to garnish.

Allspice

Is used in fruit dishes, stews, and pumpkin desserts. It tastes like a combination of cinnamon, nutmeg, and cloves and is sold ground or whole.

Ginger

Comes from a root. The fresh variety is used in many Chinese and Japanese savory dishes. The dried, ground variety is used for soups, curries, meats, and baked goods.

LET'S TALK WINE

Wine with Food

Storing

Wine should be stored in a cool place with a consistent temperature of 45°and 65°. Do not turn or move stored wine.

To prevent corks from drying out and air from entering bottles, store wine on its side. Do not store wine for long periods of time at room temperature. The higher the storage temperature, the faster to wine ages.

Cooking With Wine

Wines of all sorts are used in cooking. Special cooking wines are available in supermarkets and are not recommended because they are often inferior in quality and contain salt. Leftover drinking wine can be used in most recipes that call for wine, although adjustments in the amount of liquid may be required.

Serving

While pairing your wine with your perfect dish, it is important to serve the wine at the appropriate temperature. White Wine is best served at 50°. Place in your refrigerator two hours before serving. Store Red Wine in a cool place or chill it for fifteen minutes before serving.

FOOD CATEGORY & TYPES OF WINE

HOT & SPICY
Riesling & Chenin Blanc

TART & ACID FOOD
Chardonnay, Sauvignon Blanc

RICH FOODS
Cabernet Sauvignon, Merlot

SMOKED FOODS
Pinot Noir, Riesling

SPECIFIC FOODS & TYPE OF WINE

BEEF, LAMB
Cabernet Sauvignon, Merlot

CHICKEN, PORK, VEAL
Riesling

FISH LEAN
Chardonnay

PASTA WITH TOMATO SAUCE
Zinfandel

PASTA WITH VEGGIES
Riesling

SHELLFISH
Sauvignon Blanc

If music be the food of love, play on

—William Shakespeare

If you are not in a good mood, the only thing you should make is a Reservation

—Carla Hall

For The Love of Cooking

How do you fall in love with cooking?

1. **Familiarize yourself with the basics.**

   If you have never cooked before and do not know where to start, consider signing up for a beginner's cooking class.

2. **Start with individual recipes.**

   Start slow. Use online resources and get a better feel of recipes you are interested in preparing and eating regularly.

3. **Experiment with ingredients.**

   When you are first starting out, even if you cook occasionally but not on a regular basis, stick to ingredients you are already familiar with. Once you have given yourself time to get more comfortable in the kitchen, start adding ingredients and recipes you are less familiar with. This simple act can take you from the norm to being excited in the kitchen.

4. **Get family and friends involved.**

   Do your friends like to cook? If they do not, offer to teach them how to make your new favorite recipes. If they do like to cook, ask them to teach you how to make their favorite recipe.

Jamila LaCosta

The dread of cooking and lack of basic food preparation skills is a widespread problem but, fortunately, there is a simple solution. You do not have to be an experienced chef to prepare healthy and gourmet meals. Allow yourself the freedom to be creative and grant yourself permission to FALL IN LOVE WITH COOKING.

American

Cheese is a mild, processed, cheddar type cheese often sold in slices. This cheese is perfect for cheeseburgers.

Blue

Cheese is a sharp cheese that has an aromatic and strong flavor, which increases with age.

Brie

Cheese is a creamy French cheese with an edible white rind. Brie is used in cooking and in appetizers.

Cheddar

Cheese is a firm white to orange cheese with a flavor ranging from mild to sharp.

It is great shredded over salad, melted over fresh green vegetables, or used in sauces.

Colby

Cheese is the Wisconsin-made version of Cheddar.

It has a mild and sweet flavor. It is often used in cooking, for snacking, or on sandwiches.

WHO SAYS CUTE GIRLS CAN'T COOK?

Cream

Cheese is a smooth, spreadable, ripened fresh cheese made from cow's milk.

Cream cheese is most often used for baked cheesecake, dips and spreading.

Feta

Cheese has a tangy, sharp, and salty flavor. It is made from goat's milk. Quite common in Greek cooking, feta is often used as a salad topping.

Goat

Cheese is made from pure goat's milk.

It has a tart, tangy, and mild flavor. With age, the flavor is stronger and the texture is drier. Goat cheese is often baked, served on bread, or used as a salad topping.

Monterey Jack

Cheese gets its name from Monterey, California. It is a mild, buttery, semisoft cheese made from cow's milk.

It is sometimes flavored with peppers and garlic and often used in Tex-Mex cooking.

Jamila LaCosta

Mozzarella

Cheese is a mild, stringy cheese made from cow's milk.

Factory-produced mozzarella is semisoft and chewy with a mild flavor, while the fresh variety has a soft texture and a sweet, mild flavor.

It is commonly used on pizza and in lasagna.

Muenster

Cheese is pale yellow with small holes and an orange rind.

It is mild in flavor, while European Muenster is more pungent.

Kids love it as a snack or as a sandwich topping.

Parmesan

Cheese is an Italian hard cheese usually aged to a dry, crumbly texture. Parmesan is pleasantly sharp with a salty flavor.

It is excellent for grating over pasta sauce and salads.

Provolone

Cheese is a farm Italian cheese with a mild, smoky taste.

It is great for cooking and on sandwiches.

Ricotta

Cheese is a soft, fresh, white Italian cheese, with a sweet, mellow taste.

It is often baked in cheesecakes, lasagna, and manicotti.

Swiss

Cheese is a generic name for a group of pale-yellow cheese with large holes. They have mild, nutty flavors and firm, slightly dry textures.

Swiss is often used in cooking and is a much loved sandwich topping.

Havarti

Havarti or cream Havarti is a semisoft Danish cow's milk cheese.

It is a table cheese that can be sliced, grilled, or melted.

TOUGH COOKIE

COOKIE TIPS

GIRLUCUTEBUTCANUCOOK.com

Cookie varieties are divided into five basic types; bar, drop, refrigerated, rolled, and shaped. These types are determined by the consistency of the dough and how it is formed into cookies.

Remove butter, margarine, and cream cheese from the refrigerator to soften prior to baking.

For even baking and browning of cookies, bake them in the center of the oven. If the heat distribution in your oven is uneven, turn the baking sheet halfway through the baking time.

Preheat the oven to desired temperature about fifteen minutes before beginning to bake. For even baking and browning, place only one baking sheet at a time in the center of the oven. Allow at least 2 inches of space between the baking sheet and the wall of the oven for proper air circulation.

When baking more than one sheet of cookies at a time, rotate them from the top rack to the bottom rack halfway through the baking time.

Unbaked cookie dough can be refrigerated for up to two weeks or frozen up to six weeks. Label the dough with baking information and the date for convenience.

Most cookies bake quickly and should be watched to avoid over baking.

Check them at the minimum baking time, then watch them carefully to make sure they do not burn. Check for doneness using the tests given in the recipe.

Colored sugars, sprinkles, and candies are a fun and easy way to dress up and decorate cookies.

BAKING SECRETS

Always read the entire recipe before you begin, to ensure you have the necessary ingredients and utensils.

Use the Pan size specified in each recipe, and prepare it as directed.

Measure the ingredients accurately and assemble them in the order they are listed in the recipe.

When baking cakes, do not open the oven during the 1st half of the baking time. Cold air will interfere with the rising of the cake.

The best method for determining if a cake is done is to insert a toothpick or cake tester into the center of the cake. The cake is done if the toothpick comes out clean and dry.

Your cakes will have a more professional look, if you apply a thin layer of frosting to seal in any crumbs, and then apply a thick layer after the thin coating has set.

Oven temperatures can vary significantly depending on the manufacturer, so watch the cake carefully, and check for doneness using the test given in the recipe.

WHO SAYS CUTE GIRLS CAN'T COOK?

Place the cake pan or pans in the center of your preheated oven. Oven racks may need to be set lower for cakes baked in tube pans. If two racks are used, arrange them so they divide the oven into thirds, and then stagger the pans so one is not directly over another.

Fill the pan with batter and place it in a preheated oven.

Cake batter should not sit before baking because chemical leaveners begin working as soon as they are mixed with liquids, and the air in foam batters will begin to dissipate.

Grilling & Barbecue Basics

Always position the grill on a heat-proof surface away from trees. Make sure the grill vents are not clogged up with ashes prior to starting a fire.

To avoid flare ups and charred foods when grilling, trim meat of excess fat.

It will be best to keep a water spray bottle near your grill to quench flare ups.

The best method to determine the doneness of large cuts of meat is to use a meat thermometer.

Never, I repeat, NEVER use alcohol, gasoline or kerosene as a lighter fluid starter. All three can cause an explosion.

To start your fire and to get it going, place two or three additional coals and a small metal can and add lighter fluid. Then, stack them on the coals in the grill and light with a match.

Remember that hot coals create a hot grill, tools, and food. Always wear oven mitts to protect your hands.

The number of coals required for barbecuing depends on the size and type of grill and the amount of food that you are going to prepare.

Side note: It takes about 30 coals to grill a pound of meat.

Always serve cooked meat and poultry on a clean platter, not the one that held the raw food.

Grilling Methods

Direct Cooking Method

Food is placed on the grill directly over the coals. Make sure there is enough charcoal in a single layer to extend 1 to 2 inches beyond the area of the food. This method is for steaks, chops, hamburgers, kebab, as well as for cooking fish fast.

Indirect Cooking Method

Food is placed on the grill over a metal or disposable foil drip pan, with the coals banked either to one side or on both sides of the pan. This method is for slow, even cooking of food, such as large cuts of meat and whole chickens.

When grilling by indirect cooking for more than 45 minutes, extra briquets will need to be added to maintain a constant temperature.

Foil Wrap Method

Foods can be wrapped in foil adding vegetables, the sauce or any small amount of liquid and placed on the grill. This will help the food cook faster and keep it moist.

Making Marinades & Sauces

Marinades enhance the flavor of food, and those with acid ingredients help tenderize tougher cuts of meat.

Heavy duty, resealable plastic bags are ideal to hold foods as they marinate. Turn marinated foods occasionally to let the flavor penetrate evenly.

Marinate foods in the refrigerator, not at room temperature.

Never baste foods during the last five minutes of grilling with a marinade that was used on a raw meat, poultry, or seafood item and was not boiled afterwards. Marinades can be used as basting and dipping sauces after the food is removed by boiling them for a minimum of one minute. This will kill any harmful bacteria that may have contaminated the marinades.

Basting sauces containing sugar, honey or tomato products should be applied near the end of the grilling process, in order to prevent the food from charring.

Jamila LaCosta

Basting sauces made from seasoned oils and butters may be brushed on throughout grilling. Oils and butter prevent leaner cuts of meat from drying out.

Checking Charcoal Temperature

Whether you are cooking vegetables or steaks on the grill, use the temperature called for in the recipe. A quick easy way to estimate the temperature of the coals is to hold your hand, palm side down, about 4 inches above the coals.

Count the number of seconds you can hold your hand in that position before the heat forces you to pull it away.

Seconds	Coal Temperature
2	Hot, 375
3	Medium-hot 350
4	Medium 300
5	Low 200-250

Oh, dearie, dainty doesn't do it in the kitchen

—Julia Child

#WHOSAYSCUTEGIRLSCANTCOOK
Grocery List

Veggies/Fruits

Seafood

Dairy

Meats

Grain

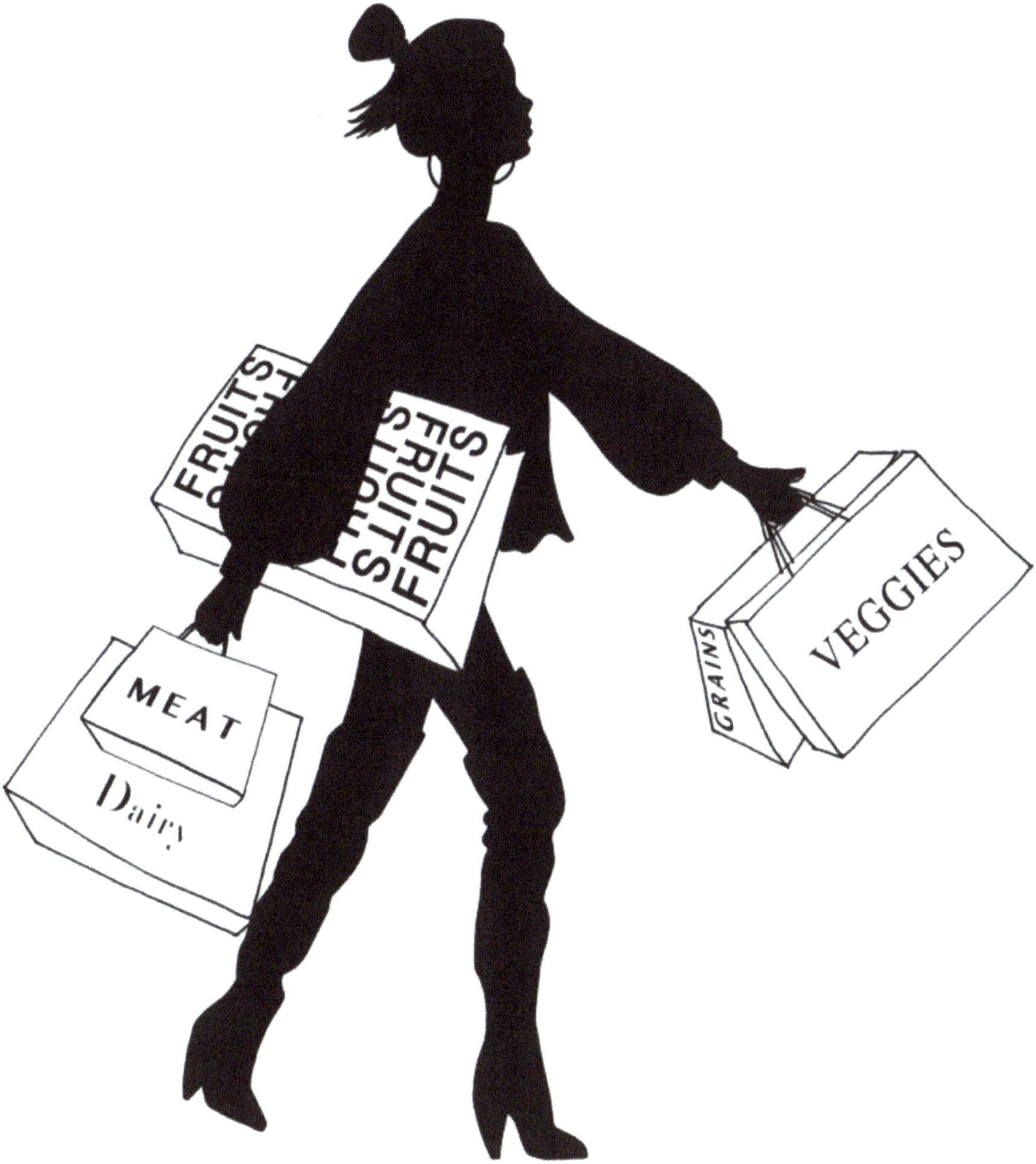
FRUITS
FRUITS
FRUITS
MEAT
Dairy
GRAINS
VEGGIES

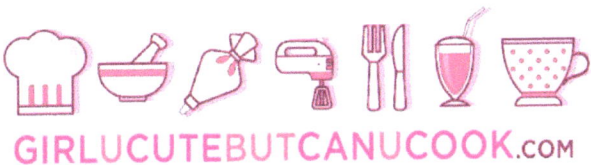

 **Recipe for**

NAME OF DISH

FROM THE KITCHEN OF

INGREDIENTS

SERVES

PREP TIME

TOTAL TIME

OVEN TEMP

DIRECTIONS

Cook with Love....
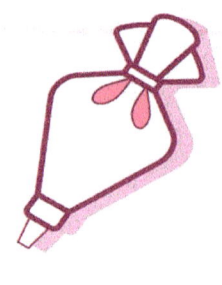

CREATED BY _____

INSERT RECIPE PHOTO

HINTS & NOTES

When Life gives you Lemons, order the Lobster Tail

—Ziad K. Abdelnour

Recipe for

NAME OF DISH

FROM THE KITCHEN OF

INGREDIENTS

SERVES

PREP TIME

TOTAL TIME

OVEN TEMP

DIRECTIONS

Cook with Love....

CREATED BY _____

INSERT RECIPE PHOTO

HINTS & NOTES

Lord, bless the recipes in this book and give us the love & patience to master them. Amen

—Prophetess Trina Reese

Recipe for

NAME OF DISH

FROM THE KITCHEN OF

INGREDIENTS

SERVES

PREP TIME

TOTAL TIME

OVEN TEMP

DIRECTIONS

Cook with Love....

CREATED BY _____

INSERT RECIPE PHOTO

HINTS & NOTES

Love to Eat? Learn how to Cook

—Jamila Rawlins

Recipe for

NAME OF DISH

FROM THE KITCHEN OF

INGREDIENTS

SERVES

PREP TIME

TOTAL TIME

OVEN TEMP

DIRECTIONS

Cook with Love....

CREATED BY _____

INSERT RECIPE PHOTO

HINTS & NOTES

I don't feel like cooking this shit right now!

— Shayla LaCosta

 # Recipe for

NAME OF DISH

FROM THE KITCHEN OF

INGREDIENTS

SERVES

PREP TIME

TOTAL TIME

OVEN TEMP

DIRECTIONS

Cook with Love....

CREATED BY _____

INSERT RECIPE PHOTO

HINTS & NOTES

THE 3 P'S TO COOKING

Patience

Passion

Practice

NAME OF DISH

FROM THE KITCHEN OF

INGREDIENTS

SERVES

PREP TIME

TOTAL TIME

OVEN TEMP

DIRECTIONS

Cook with Love....

CREATED BY _____

INSERT RECIPE PHOTO

HINTS & NOTES

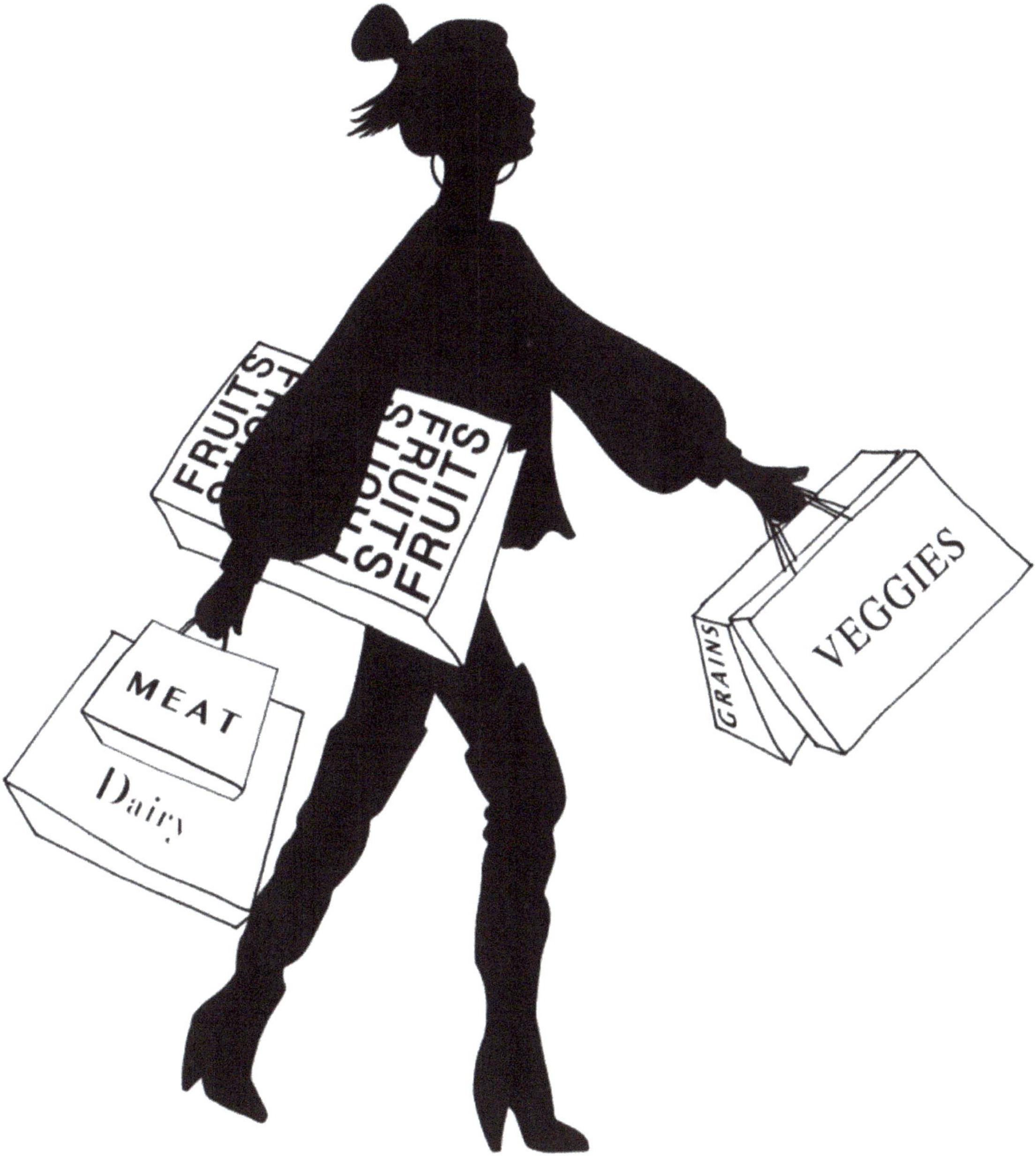
FRUITS
FRUITS
FRUITS
FRUITS
MEAT
Dairy
GRAINS
VEGGIES

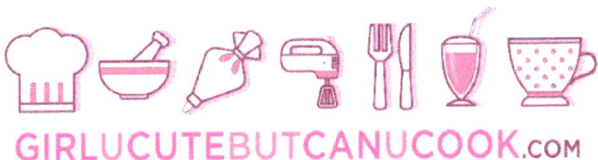

#WHOSAYSCUTEGIRLSCANTCOOK
Grocery List

Veggies/Fruits

Seafood

Dairy

Meats

Grain

 # Recipe for

NAME OF DISH

FROM THE KITCHEN OF

INGREDIENTS

SERVES

PREP TIME

TOTAL TIME

OVEN TEMP

DIRECTIONS

Cook with Love....

CREATED BY _____

INSERT RECIPE PHOTO

HINTS & NOTES

The Best Dishes are cooked with love

—Sharmin Rucker

Recipe for

NAME OF DISH

FROM THE KITCHEN OF

INGREDIENTS

SERVES
PREP TIME
TOTAL TIME
OVEN TEMP

DIRECTIONS

Cook with Love....

CREATED BY _____

INSERT RECIPE PHOTO

HINTS & NOTES

Kitchen Rules

If it smells, throw it away

If it's dirty, wash it

If you take it out, put it away

If it's on, turn it off

# Recipe for

NAME OF DISH

FROM THE KITCHEN OF

INGREDIENTS

SERVES

PREP TIME

TOTAL TIME

OVEN TEMP

DIRECTIONS

Cook with Love....

CREATED BY _____

| INSERT RECIPE PHOTO |

HINTS & NOTES

I am proud of the chef I am today because I went through one hell of a time becoming one

-Tiara LaCosta

Recipe for

NAME OF DISH

FROM THE KITCHEN OF

INGREDIENTS

SERVES

PREP TIME

TOTAL TIME

OVEN TEMP

DIRECTIONS

Cook with Love....

CREATED BY _____

INSERT RECIPE PHOTO

HINTS & NOTES

Let's face it, a nice creamy chocolate cake does a lot for a lot of people; it does for me

—Audrey Hepburn

 **Recipe for**

NAME OF DISH

FROM THE KITCHEN OF

INGREDIENTS

SERVES

PREP TIME

TOTAL TIME

OVEN TEMP

DIRECTIONS

Cook with Love....

CREATED BY _____

INSERT RECIPE PHOTO

HINTS & NOTES

I love cooking!
It's my peaceful time
to put love into all
the dishes that are
prepared.
So while I cook
please stay out!!!

—Sonya Meadows

 **Recipe for**

NAME OF DISH

FROM THE KITCHEN OF

INGREDIENTS

SERVES

PREP TIME

TOTAL TIME

OVEN TEMP

DIRECTIONS

Cook with Love....

CREATED BY _____

INSERT RECIPE PHOTO

HINTS & NOTES

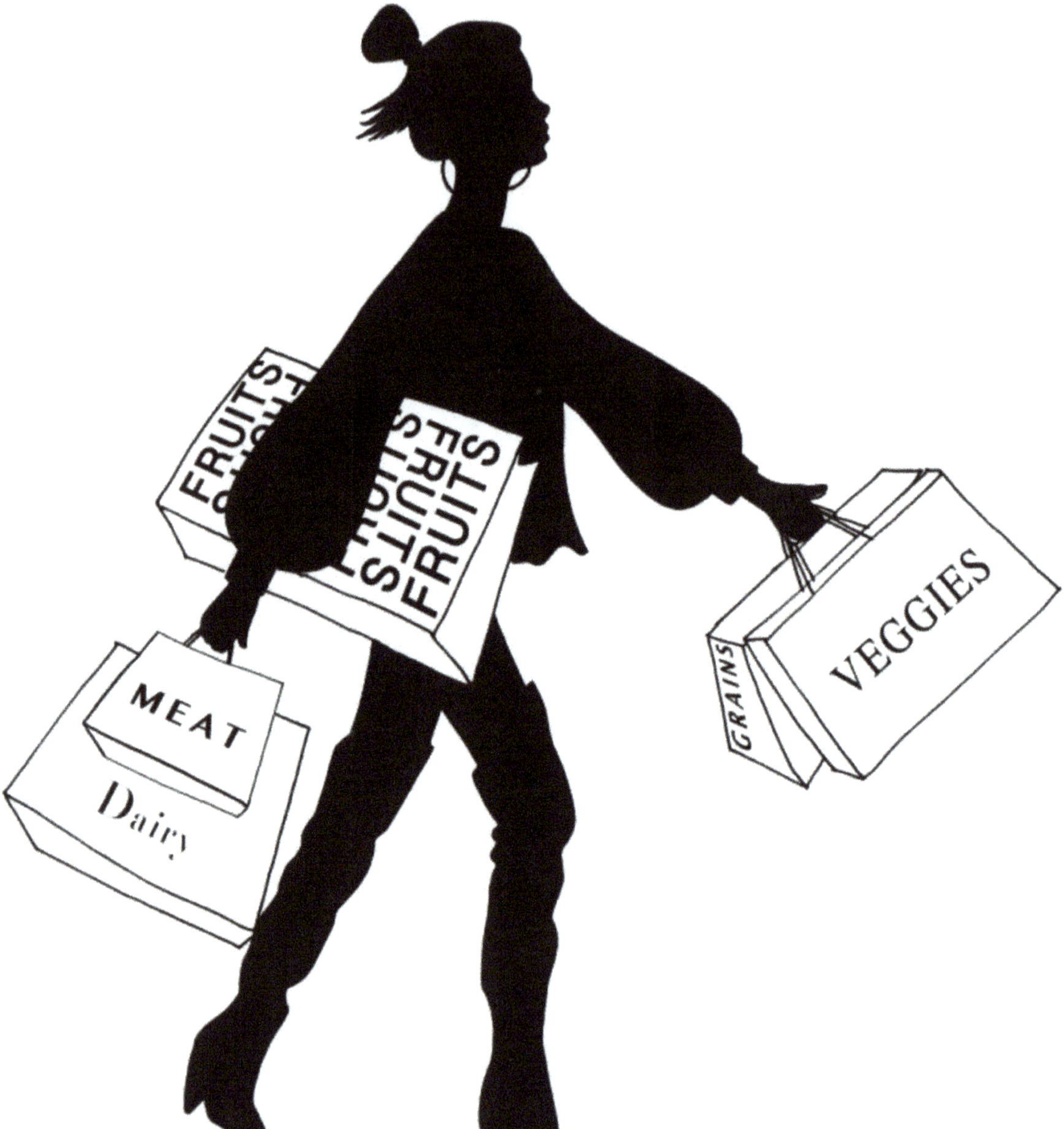

GIRLUCUTEBUTCANUCOOK.COM

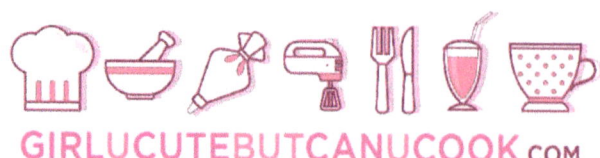

#WHOSAYSCUTEGIRLSCANTCOOK
Grocery List

Veggies/Fruits

Seafood

Dairy

Meats

Grain

 **Recipe for**

NAME OF DISH

FROM THE KITCHEN OF

INGREDIENTS

SERVES
PREP TIME
TOTAL TIME
OVEN TEMP

DIRECTIONS

Cook with Love....

CREATED BY _____

INSERT RECIPE PHOTO

HINTS & NOTES

 Recipe for

NAME OF DISH

FROM THE KITCHEN OF

INGREDIENTS

SERVES

PREP TIME

TOTAL TIME

OVEN TEMP

DIRECTIONS

Cook with Love....

CREATED BY _____

INSERT RECIPE PHOTO

HINTS & NOTES

# Recipe for

NAME OF DISH

FROM THE KITCHEN OF

INGREDIENTS

SERVES

PREP TIME

TOTAL TIME

OVEN TEMP

DIRECTIONS

Cook with Love....

CREATED BY _____

INSERT RECIPE PHOTO

HINTS & NOTES

Recipe for

NAME OF DISH

FROM THE KITCHEN OF

INGREDIENTS

SERVES
PREP TIME
TOTAL TIME
OVEN TEMP

DIRECTIONS

Cook with Love....

CREATED BY _____

INSERT RECIPE PHOTO

HINTS & NOTES

Recipe for

NAME OF DISH

FROM THE KITCHEN OF

INGREDIENTS

SERVES

PREP TIME

TOTAL TIME

OVEN TEMP

DIRECTIONS

Cook with Love....

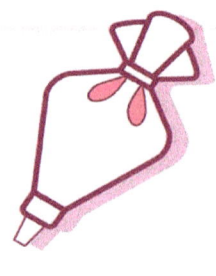

CREATED BY _____

INSERT RECIPE PHOTO

HINTS & NOTES

People who love 2 Eat R always the best people

—Julia Child

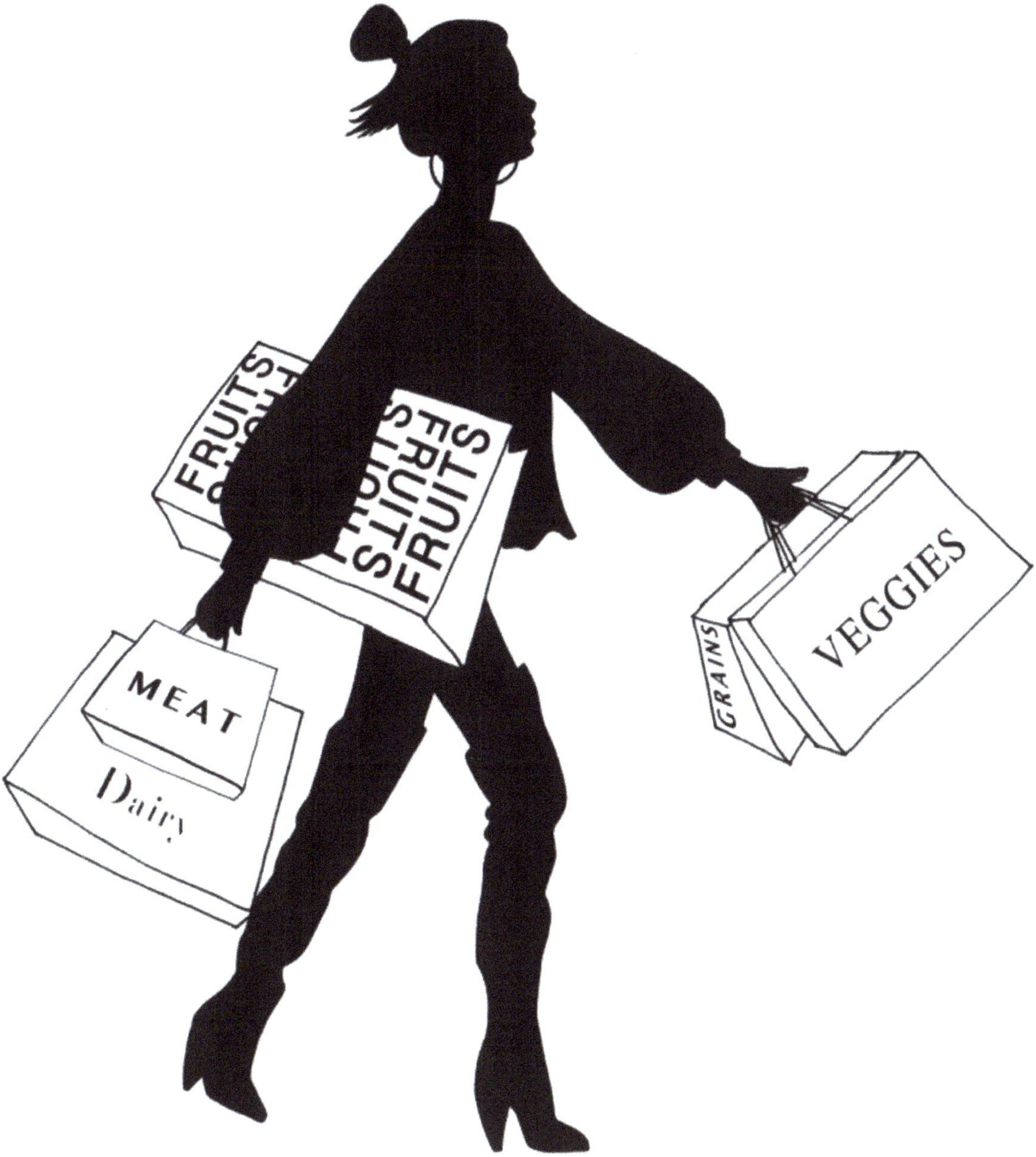

GIRLUCUTEBUTCANUCOOK.COM

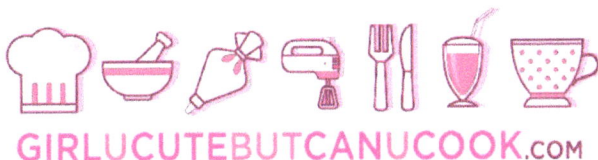

#WHOSAYSCUTEGIRLSCANTCOOK
Grocery List

Veggies/Fruits

Seafood

Dairy

Meats

Grain

"Cooking is like love. It should be entered into with abandon or not at all.
-Harriet Van Horne

Cooking Ideas

As busy as I am I will always find the time to make my family a wonderful meal.

"To eat is a necessity, but to eat intelligently is an art"

—Francois Dela Rochefoucald

Gourmet Cooking

Cooking with Wine

"How she loved a man who would fit his life around the seasoning needs of a fish".

-Susan May Warren

Cooking for Bae

"The way to a man's heart is through his stomach"

Grilling means good times, good friends, and great food.

Let the Grill Begin

Keep it Cute on the Grill

Not all girls are made of sugar & spice and everything nice.
Some girls are made of sarcasm and wine and everything fine.

Girls Night Out

Being the host & the cook on girls night is always a great feeling

"I don't know what it is about food your mother makes for you, especially when it's something that anyone can make — pancakes, meat loaf, tuna salad — but it carries a certain taste of memory."
— Mitch Albom

Holiday Cooking

The Love of Cooking

Creativity can be delicious

Creative Cooking

The love of creating mix it & recreate it

You can never get
a cup of tea
large enough
or a book
long enough
to suit me.

C.S. Lewis

Meditate & Tea

Tea & Thoughts

Beauty & Brunch

invite the girls over for a fun brunch discussing beauty, beauty products and share your reviews & ideas over good food & mimosas.

1. plan event
2. theme
3. food
4. cocktails
5. attendees
6. date & time
7. supplies

Beauty & Brunch

In this space create your event

Vision with a twist

create a vision board event, invite the family and friends over to participate with their dreams and goals over a great meal. or hors d'oeuvres and mocktails.

1. theme
2. food
3. Mocktails
4. attendees
5..date & time
6. supplies

Vision with a twist

In this space create your event

Paint Bae

invite the girls or bae & his friends over for a BBQ, while listening to some cool jams, while painting your favorite image on your canvas, while sipping Prosecco under the stars

1. plan event
2. food
3. cocktails
4. attendees
5. date & time
6. supplies

Paint Bae

in this space create your event

Your dish is like your palet, make it a work of art

~A. Neff King

#WHOSAYSCUTEGIRLSCANTCOOK
Grocery List

Veggies/Fruits

Seafood

Dairy

Meats

Grain

GIRLUCUTEBUTCANUCOOK.COM

 # Recipe for

NAME OF DISH

FROM THE KITCHEN OF

INGREDIENTS

SERVES
PREP TIME
TOTAL TIME
OVEN TEMP

DIRECTIONS

Cook with Love....

CREATED BY _____

INSERT RECIPE PHOTO

HINTS & NOTES

I love making meals with only the ingredients in my refrigerator

-Mom/Grandma

#WHOSAYSCUTEGIRLSCANTCOOK
Grocery List

Veggies/Fruits

Seafood

Dairy

Meats

Grain

NAME OF DISH

FROM THE KITCHEN OF

INGREDIENTS

SERVES

PREP TIME

TOTAL TIME

OVEN TEMP

DIRECTIONS

Cook with Love....

CREATED BY _____

INSERT RECIPE PHOTO

HINTS & NOTES

The best comfort food will always be greens, cornbread, & fried chicken

—Maya Angelou

#WHOSAYSCUTEGIRLSCANTCOOK
Grocery List

Veggies/Fruits

Seafood

Dairy

Meats

Grain

girlucutebutcanucook.com

 **Recipe for**

NAME OF DISH

FROM THE KITCHEN OF

INGREDIENTS

SERVES

PREP TIME

TOTAL TIME

OVEN TEMP

DIRECTIONS

Cook with Love....

CREATED BY _____

INSERT RECIPE PHOTO

HINTS & NOTES

Cooking is about creating something delicious for someone else.
— Ayumi Komura

#WHOSAYSCUTEGIRLSCANTCOOK
Grocery List

Veggies/Fruits

Seafood

Dairy

Meats

Grain

girlcutebutcanucook.com

NAME OF DISH

FROM THE KITCHEN OF

INGREDIENTS

SERVES
PREP TIME
TOTAL TIME
OVEN TEMP

DIRECTIONS

Cook with Love....

CREATED BY _____

INSERT RECIPE PHOTO

HINTS & NOTES

I love 2 Bake it because you can set it & forget it

—Joan Millien

#WHOSAYSCUTEGIRLSCANTCOOK
Grocery List

Veggies/Fruits

Seafood

Dairy

Meats

Grain

girlcutebutcanscook.com

 Recipe for

NAME OF DISH

FROM THE KITCHEN OF

INGREDIENTS

SERVES

PREP TIME

TOTAL TIME

OVEN TEMP

DIRECTIONS

Cook with Love....

CREATED BY _____

INSERT RECIPE PHOTO

HINTS & NOTES

The star ingredient that goes into every dish I make is LOVE and it taste so good!

—Charmaine Webster

#WHOSAYSCUTEGIRLSCANTCOOK
Grocery List

Veggies/Fruits

Seafood

Dairy

Meats

Grain

GIRLUCUTEBUTCANUCOOK.COM

 **Recipe for**

NAME OF DISH

FROM THE KITCHEN OF

INGREDIENTS

SERVES

PREP TIME

TOTAL TIME

OVEN TEMP

DIRECTIONS

Cook with Love....

CREATED BY _____

INSERT RECIPE PHOTO

HINTS & NOTES

Somehow I made it through life without measuring a thing! I 'eyeball' all of my ingredients. My dishes come out perfect everytime!

—Shonda McDowell

#WHOSAYSCUTEGIRLSCANTCOOK
Grocery List

Veggies/Fruits

Seafood

Dairy

Meats

Grain

 # Recipe for

NAME OF DISH

FROM THE KITCHEN OF

INGREDIENTS

SERVES

PREP TIME

TOTAL TIME

OVEN TEMP

DIRECTIONS

Cook with Love....

CREATED BY _____

INSERT RECIPE PHOTO

HINTS & NOTES

Recipe life

Recipes from love

HOME-COOKED MEALS

SEASON IT JUST RIGHT!

Essential kitchen spices for more flavorful dishes!

ecipe for

NAME OF DISH

FROM THE KITCHEN OF

INGREDIENTS

SERVES
PREP TIME
TOTAL TIME
OVEN TEMP

DIRECTIONS

Cook with Love....

CREATED BY _____

INSERT RECIPE PHOTO

HINTS & NOTES

Recipe for

NAME OF DISH

FROM THE KITCHEN OF

INGREDIENTS

SERVES

PREP TIME

TOTAL TIME

OVEN TEMP

DIRECTIONS

Cook with Love....

CREATED BY _____

INSERT RECIPE PHOTO

HINTS & NOTES

Recipe for

NAME OF DISH

FROM THE KITCHEN OF

INGREDIENTS

SERVES

PREP TIME

TOTAL TIME

OVEN TEMP

DIRECTIONS

Cook with Love....

CREATED BY _____

INSERT RECIPE PHOTO

HINTS & NOTES

 # Recipe for

NAME OF DISH

FROM THE KITCHEN OF

INGREDIENTS

SERVES

PREP TIME

TOTAL TIME

OVEN TEMP

DIRECTIONS

Cook with Love....

CREATED BY _____

INSERT RECIPE PHOTO

HINTS & NOTES

Recipes from the heart

Brunch is a combination of breakfast and lunch, and regularly has some form of alcoholic drink, mimosas, and mocktails. It is usually served any time before 3 o'clock in the afternoon. The word is a portmanteau of breakfast and lunch.

Sunday Brunch

Crazy Cute Grilled Shrimp, Scallop, Watermelon and Cucumber Arugula Salad

WHO SAYS CUTE GIRLS CAN'T COOK?

These grilled shrimp, scallop, watermelon, and cucumber Kebab sticks are packed with so many flavors. It is a sweet-and-salty combination that looks just beautiful on the table for a backyard cookout, potluck or even a Sunday Brunch!

Makes 4 Kebab Sticks

- 8 scallops
- 12 red argentine shrimp (cleaned, deveined & peeled)
- 20 cubes of cucumber
- 20 cubes of watermelon
- 1 red onion (thinly sliced)
- 1 carrot (peeled & thinly sliced)
- 4 cups of arugula
- 2 lemons (squeezed)
- 1 lime (squeezed)
- ½ cup of honey
- ½ tablespoon of minced garlic
- 2 tablespoons of soy sauce
- 1 teaspoon of red chili flakes or scotch bonnet pepper
- 1 teaspoon of season salt
- 2 sticks of chopped chives

- **Prep Time: 30 minutes**
- **Cook Time: 15 minutes**
- **Ready in: 45 minutes**

Place the honey, minced garlic, scotch pepper or chili flakes, soy sauce, squeezed lime juice, and squeezed lemon juice in a blender, cover and process until pureed.

Transfer to a small saucepan and bring to a boil, then reduce heat to medium. Cook uncovered for 10 minutes. Reduce the sauce to half and pour in a large bowl with a lid.

Place the shrimp, cucumber, watermelon, and scallops in a large bowl. Add the season salt and stir. Cover with a lid and place in the refrigerator for 30 minutes.

Using 4 wooden skewers, place the mixed food as followed: watermelon, cucumber, scallop, watermelon, cucumber, shrimp, and repeat (per skewer: 6 cubes of watermelon, 5 cubes of cucumber, 3 shrimps, 2 scallops)

Prepare the salad, clean all the veggies and pat dry with a paper towel. Use your veggie peeler to peel the top layer off and discard. Thinly slice the peeled carrot, cucumber, and red onion, then place them in a salad bowl. Add the arugula. Cover with a lid and shake it before placing the salad in the refrigerator.

Place the kebabs on an oiled rack over a medium heat grill and cover for 3 minutes on each side, till the shrimp is pink. Brush the glaze on the kebabs grill for 2 more minutes on each side.

Add the salad to a plate. Place the kebab on the side of the plate with the reserved glaze.

There are no rules 2 Cooking just follow the basic instructions or follow your instincts

BBQ & Mimosas

Jerk Pork Pineapple Kebabs

Jamila LaCosta

Perfect for summer barbecues, but just as easily made in your kitchen on a cold winter's night. BBQ on a stick. These Jamaican Jerk Pork Kebabs are a real deal breaker. **Serves 4**

- 2 packs of pork tenderloin (cleaned and cut into 1-inch cubes)
- 1 can of cubed pineapple chunks
- 1 medium red onion (cut into squares)
- 1 red pepper and 1 yellow pepper (cleaned and cut into squares)
- 1 carrot (cleaned, peeled, and cut into squares)
- ½ scotch bonnet pepper (chopped)
- 2 tbsp of honey
- 2 tbsp of brown sugar
- 2 tbsp of jerk seasoning
- 2 tbsp of complete seasoning
- ½ cup of melted butter
- 1 tsp of peeled & diced ginger
- 2 green onions (cleaned & chopped)
- 1 garlic clove
- 2 tbsp of garlic sauce
- 2 tbsp of coconut milk powder

WHO SAYS CUTE GIRLS CAN'T COOK?

- **Prep Time: 15 minutes**
- **Cook Time 10 minutes**
- **Soak the Kebab sticks for 30 minutes**
- **Ready in: 1 day and 55 minutes**

Combine the scotch bonnet pepper, brown sugar, honey, season salt, green onions, ginger, coconut milk powder, soy sauce and melted butter into a food processor or blender until it forms into a paste.

Pour the bags into different large Ziplock bags. Add the pork to one bag. Add the pineapple cubes and veggies to another bag. And place in your refrigerator for 24 hrs.

Heat your grill on high, add the marinated pork, veggies, and pineapple cubes in alternating layers to the kebab sticks.

Reduce the grill heat to medium. Grill the kebabs for 5 minutes per side, until the pork is done.

Mocktails
A cocktail without the alcohol

Jamila LaCosta

Pomegranate Lemon Mocktail

This Pomegranate Lemon Mocktail is a refreshing summer drink recipe. Its citrus and sweet at the same time and great as a refresher.

This Pomegranate Lemon Mocktail is a super tropical cocktail perfect for summer.

- *1 cup of pineapple juice*
- *1 cup of lemonade*
- *½ of pomegranate juice*
- *1 tbsp simple syrup*
- *Lemon wedges to decorate the glass*

Grab a glass pitcher and pour the pineapple juice, lemonade, pomegranate juice, and the simple syrup.

Mix everything together.

Pour into the glasses filled with ice.

Decorate the glasses with lemon wedges on the rim and serve.

Share your Cooking...
Share your Soul......

—Jamila Rawlins

Dirty Monkey Mocktail

Made with bananas, cream, and chocolate, this frozen drink is a great option for the summer on a sunny day.

- 1 cup half and half
- 2 cups of ice
- 1 cup of vanilla soymilk
- 2 bananas peeled
- ⅓ chocolate syrup

Add all the ingredients to a blender and mix well.

Pour into some glasses, add some whipped cream, banana slices and chocolate throughout the glasses.

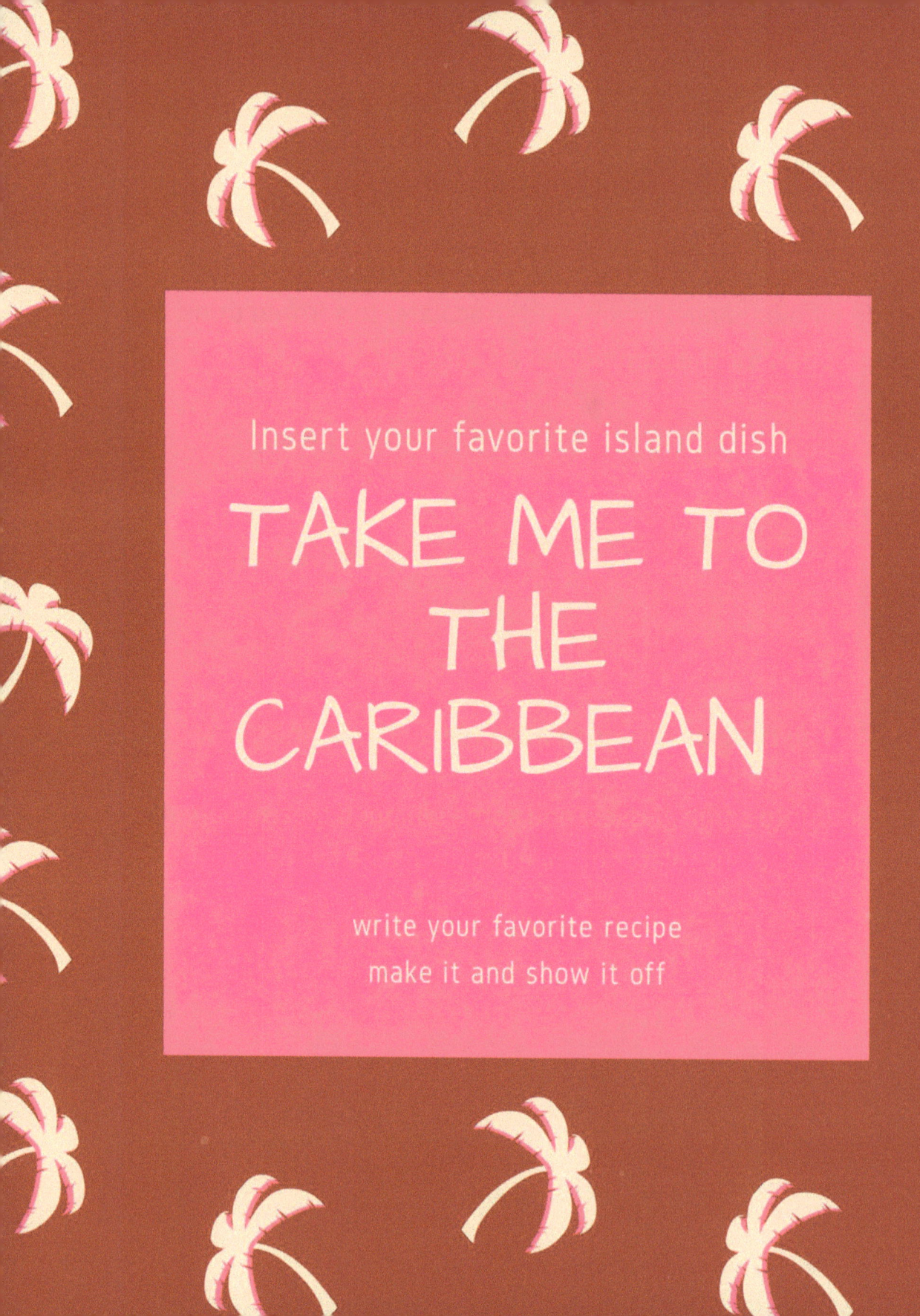

#WHOSAYSCUTEGIRLSCANTCOOK
Grocery List

Veggies/Fruits

Seafood

Dairy

Meats

Grain

Recipe for

NAME OF DISH

FROM THE KITCHEN OF

INGREDIENTS

SERVES
PREP TIME
TOTAL TIME
OVEN TEMP

DIRECTIONS

Cook with Love....

CREATED BY _____

INSERT RECIPE PHOTO

HINTS & NOTES

A Taste of Italy

Insert your favorite Italian dish

cook it & show it off

#WHOSAYSCUTEGIRLSCANTCOOK
Grocery List

Veggies/Fruits

Seafood

Dairy

Meats

Grain

 # Recipe for

NAME OF DISH

FROM THE KITCHEN OF

INGREDIENTS

SERVES

PREP TIME

TOTAL TIME

OVEN TEMP

DIRECTIONS

Cook with Love....

CREATED BY _____

INSERT RECIPE PHOTO

HINTS & NOTES

#WHOSAYSCUTEGIRLSCANTCOOK
Grocery List

Veggies/Fruits

Seafood

Dairy

Meats

Grain

 # Recipe for

NAME OF DISH

FROM THE KITCHEN OF

INGREDIENTS

SERVES

PREP TIME

TOTAL TIME

OVEN TEMP

DIRECTIONS

Cook with Love....

CREATED BY _____

INSERT RECIPE PHOTO

HINTS & NOTES

Appetizers

a small dish of food

or a drink taken before

a meal or the main course

of a meal to stimulate

one's appetite.

Recipe for

NAME OF DISH

FROM THE KITCHEN OF

INGREDIENTS

SERVES

PREP TIME

TOTAL TIME

OVEN TEMP

DIRECTIONS

Cook with Love....

CREATED BY _____

INSERT RECIPE PHOTO

HINTS & NOTES

Soups

&

Salads

Soup is typically thought of as a liquid dish consisting of some type of meat and vegetables in a broth. Salad is typically thought of as a cold dish full of leafy greens and vegetables tossed in some type of dressing

Recipe for

NAME OF DISH

FROM THE KITCHEN OF

INGREDIENTS

- **SERVES**
- **PREP TIME**
- **TOTAL TIME**
- **OVEN TEMP**

DIRECTIONS

Cook with Love....

CREATED BY _____

INSERT RECIPE PHOTO

HINTS & NOTES

Main Course

the main course is the featured or primary dish in a meal consisting of several courses. It usually follows the entrée course.

Recipe for

NAME OF DISH

FROM THE KITCHEN OF

INGREDIENTS

SERVES
PREP TIME
TOTAL TIME
OVEN TEMP

DIRECTIONS

Cook with Love....

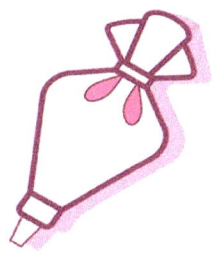

CREATED BY _____

INSERT RECIPE PHOTO

HINTS & NOTES

Side Dishes

a dish served as subsidiary to the main one.

 **Recipe for**

NAME OF DISH

FROM THE KITCHEN OF

INGREDIENTS

SERVES

PREP TIME

TOTAL TIME

OVEN TEMP

DIRECTIONS

Cook with Love....

CREATED BY _____

INSERT RECIPE PHOTO

HINTS & NOTES

Desserts

the sweet course eaten at

the end of a meal.

**Recipe for**

NAME OF DISH

FROM THE KITCHEN OF

INGREDIENTS

SERVES

PREP TIME

TOTAL TIME

OVEN TEMP

DIRECTIONS

Cook with Love....

CREATED BY _____

INSERT RECIPE PHOTO

HINTS & NOTES

Creative Dishes

Think Gourmet Meals, Not Magic Moments

ecipe for

NAME OF DISH

FROM THE KITCHEN OF

INGREDIENTS

SERVES
PREP TIME
TOTAL TIME
OVEN TEMP

DIRECTIONS

Cook with Love....

CREATED BY _____

INSERT RECIPE PHOTO

HINTS & NOTES

Q What are your favorite things to cook?

insert photos & recipes

Q Do you meal prep your meals for the week or do you go out to eat every week?

insert notes & recipes

Snack Time

WHO SAYS CUTE GIRLS CAN'T COOK?

Hennessey Caramel Popcorn. Crunchy popcorn coated with a Hennessey caramel sauce. Great for movie night, holiday parties, and homemade gifts.

Caramel is the essence of fall and summer and this recipe hits that summer start button. It is a sweet treat that makes movie night with bae or your girlfriends more fun and holiday parties more magical.

This is a real and easy fun way to make this popcorn.

- *4 bags of microwave popcorn*
- *¾ salted butter*
- *1 cup of brown sugar*
- *1 cup of simple syrup*
- *1 cup of caramel syrup*
- *1 teaspoon baking soda*
- *2 tablespoons of Hennessey*

Line your baking sheets with parchment paper.

Pop your bags of popcorn in the microwave.

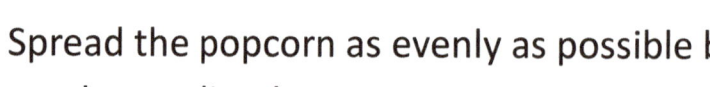

Spread the popcorn as evenly as possible between your parchment lined pans.

Heat oven to 250 degrees.

Add the butter, brown sugar, simple syrup, and caramel syrup into a 3-quart saucepan. Place over a medium high flame. Stir until the butter has melted and the mixture starts to bubble.

Add the baking soda and the Hennessey.

Stir the mixture with a wooden spoon. Use your spoon to drizzle the Hennessey Caramel on your popcorn.

Once you have all your mixture drizzled on the popcorn, put in the oven for 15 minutes. Set your timer.

After 15 minutes remove one pan from oven and stir the popcorn using your wooden spoon. Slide the spatula between the popcorn and the parchment paper and gently flip the popcorn over. Make sure you are scraping the settled caramel off the parchment paper and turning it back onto the popcorn.

Pull the second tray of popcorn out and replace it with the batch you just stirred. Stir the second pan in the same way you stirred the first, then place the pan back into the oven. The pan that was on top should now be on the bottom and vice versa.

Set the timer for 15 minutes, then set up a workspace with wax paper.

When the timer goes off, remove the first pan from the oven. Carefully grab the parchment paper by one corner of the pan and gently roll the whole sheet, popcorn and all, upside down onto one end of the wax paper. Use the spatula to scrape off any bits remaining in the corner of the pan, then peel the parchment paper off of the popcorn. Do not scrape the caramel off the parchment. Instead, lay the paper flat to cool.

Repeat the process with the second pan of popcorn, dumping it next to but not on top of the first batch.

By this point the first batch will be cool enough to touch. Gently break apart any large clumps of popcorn so that you have small clusters of yummy goodness.

Repeat, then leave the whole thing to cool for at least 30 minutes.

Your popcorn can last up to at least two weeks at room temperature in an airtight container or plastic bag.

Keep it Cute sis

Acknowledgements

To all the cuties who love to cook or who love to learn different recipes and techniques.

I would love to thank my mother for putting up with me during the long hours of creating this recipe journal.

My beautiful Dashaun, for giving me so many ideas for the millennials and his amazing creative direction.

My youthful and beautiful Brianna, thank you for being the model and big cheerleader you are. If I asked you to participate, you never told me no.

My grateful and loving sister, thank you for allowing me to take over yours and mom's house, while putting this journal together.

To my lovely girlfriends, thank you for giving me your amazing food quotes to insert in this journal.

To all my cuties and foodies, hope you enjoy your Recipe Food Journal and fill it with all your favorite recipes.

Thank you for purchasing this journal and having fun with food.

www.ingramcontent.com/pod-product-compliance
Lightning Source LLC
Chambersburg PA
CBHW051404110526
44592CB00023B/2954